PEAK
SECRETS A...

HOME AND VILLAGE LIFE
~
CHURCHES AND CHAPELS

Lindsey Porter

Produced by
Landmark Publishing Ltd,
Waterloo House, 12 Compton, Ashbourne
Derbyshire DE6 1DA England

For the Publishers
Ashbourne Editions
Sprinkswood, Clifton, Ashbourne,
Derbyshire DE6 2GL

1st Edition

© **Lindsey Porter 1999**

Printers: Cayfosa Industria Gráfica
Design: Samantha Witham

Cover Photo: The cheese press by the George Hotel, Hathersage.
Rear Cover : Longnor Market Hall; Old Grammar School, Ashbourne.

Preface

Changes in domestic life have been dramatic in both urban and rural communities. Perhaps in the latter, more examples of days gone by survive, such as pinfolds, wells, market halls, dovecotes etc. Here is a collection of interesting houses and features connected with domestic life across the Peak, from the tragic reminders of plague victims to unusual village wells and pretty village schools. There is also a chapter on Churches and Chapels which looks at some of the more unusual aspects of these buildings.

If you have enjoyed this book look out for books 2 and 3 at your bookseller or use the order form at the end of the book to order them by mail order.

Below: Perhaps the oldest school building in the area is the former Queen Elizabeth's Grammar School in Ashbourne. It dates from 1585 and this building was used by the school until 1993, a remarkable record. The trustees of the building finally sold it in December 1997. The school was in the middle with a master's house at each end. Even the cobblestones on the pavement are protected — they were fetched from the River Dove centuries ago!

Opposite: Riber Castle, built between 1862-68 by John Smedley as his residence. Smedley owned the huge hydro which is now the County Offices in Matlock. The castle dominates the skyline from Matlock and its publicity value could not have escaped him. It is now a ruin with a zoo set in the grounds.

PEAK DISTRICT SECRETS AND CURIOSITIES

1

Lindsey Porter

Ashbourne Editions

Home and Village Life

Churches and Chapels

Baslow

Above left: Old Hall Hotel at Buxton. The original hall survives intact and is the part in the middle, now faced by two bays. This was where Mary, Queen of Scots resided when she came here to take the waters. She came five times between 1572 and 1583.

Above right: Tucked away in the centre of Winster is the Georgian Hall. Unusual for the Peak, it has a flat roof and balustrade.

Left: One of the houses at Edensor. The village was rebuilt out of sight of

Chatsworth by the sixth Duke of Devonshire, between 1838-42. All the houses are different as the Duke could not decide which design to choose. Not all the village was demolished, however. The former village inn — now refaced — is the village cafe and shop **(opposite above)**. One property in the old main street remains. The owner did not wish to move, and out of consideration for the age of his tenant, the Duke allowed him to stay **(inset)**.

A contrast is the Old Hall at Fenny Bentley, north of Ashbourne **(opposite below)** which still retains its medieval tower, visible from the A515. The tower is the remnant of a fortified house that occupied a moated site. It was owned by the Beresford family and passed by marriage to Charles Cotton. An unusual monument to the Beresfords, dated 1473, may be seen in the nearby church.

Above: Hartington Hall was never anything more than a yeoman farmer's house and farm, but a very fine building it is, none the less. Until about 1951, it was the home of the Bateman family who kept a small suite of rooms. It is the oldest surviving continuously used youth hostel in the Peak, having opened in 1934. The purchase price of £10,000 was the highest public appeal by the YHA at the time. The oldest

part of the house is the south elevation, which dates from 1611. The remaining parts followed in 1861 — two years after the large range of farm buildings. Finally, the double bay on the west front was added in 1911 — 300 years after the south front had been built.

Left: Now known as the Old House Museum, this Bakewell house above the church was built in 1543. It has been restored and now displays its original wattle and daub interior walls. It was extended in about 1620 and converted into tenements by Sir Richard Arkwright in about 1790.

Opposite above: These dovecotes may be seen in the gable end of Knowsley Cross Farm, near Longnor. Doves were an important source of meat, especially in medieval times.

Opposite below: Rather than pay the ridiculous Window Tax, many householders removed windows which they felt they could manage without. This rather good example is in Stanton-in-the-Peak.

The Peak has some wonderful gardens such as Chatsworth and Haddon Hall. Less well known and perhaps the most stunning in the area is Lea Garden (**above**). It was established by John Marsden Smedley who lived in the adjacent Lea Green, a country house which is now an education centre. Smedley planted many different species of rhododendron in an old quarry over a 20 year period. Today the site has matured and over 500 species may be seen. It is open every day during the season. Lea village is near to Cromford and just to the north of Crich.

When the 16th Earl of Shrewsbury rebuilt Alton Abbey and renamed it Alton Towers, it was a result of having already created a huge garden involving a whole valley. The Earl turned conventional garden design on its head, shocking the experts of his day. Today it is a wonderful place, especially at the end of May. Unfortunately, in order to see the gardens, you have to pay to enter the Amusement Park. One of the attractions is the Chinese Pagoda fountain (**left**), as elegant now as when it was first erected.

Some of the village schools stand out because of their pleasing design. They include Ilam (**overleaf top**), built by the Watts-Russell family in 1854; the former Grammar School at Wirksworth (**overleaf bottom**), which was founded in 1576 and rebuilt in 1828; and Hollinsclough (**above**) a simply designed school with some elegant features. The latter has been replaced by an adjacent larger building.

This unusual house was built by Sir Richard Arkwright for the apprentices of his nearby cotton mill at Cressbrookdale.

The Market Place was the centre of village life and several Market Halls and crosses survive. It was necessary to have a charter to hold a market and not all villages were lucky enough to have one. Here are a few reminders.

Bakewell Market Hall was built in the early part of the seventeenth century. It is now a National Park information centre (**opposite above**). Winster's Market Hall dates from either the fifteenth or sixteenth century. The first floor was added later. This was the first Derbyshire building to be aquired by the National Trust. The arches have been infilled to strengthen the structure (**opposite below**). Ashbourne's Market Hall (**above**) was built in 1861. It is now known as the Town Hall. Originally it housed the Literary Institute and Library; Assembly Rooms (where the market stalls would have been housed); the armoury of the Dove Valley Rifle Corp and the Masonic Lodge.

Although detail relating to the granting of a charter at Longnor is obscure, this village was an important Moorland market town, on a par with Leek. The Market Hall is dated 1873. The plaque lists a "Table of Tolls payable at Longnor Markets and Fairs". It includes prices for buyers and sellers.

The market cross in the Market Place, Chapel-en-le-Frith **(right)**. The cross in the centre of Bonsall **(above left)**. The Butter Cross at Leek **(above right)**. It was originally erected by the Joliffe family in 1671 and occupied a site at the junction of Sheep Market and Stanley Street, at the bottom of the Market Place. In 1806 it was removed and ended up in the cemetery in 1857, finally being restored to the Market Place in 1986.

Tissington Well Dressing is thought to commemorate the purity and continued flow of the water supply during times when it was most needed. Elsewhere, the ceremony commenced during the nineteenth century to commemorate the provision of a supply of fresh water, such as at Wirksworth and Youlgreave. Ashbourne was behind many other local communities in bringing fresh water to the town. In 1883 there was an outbreak of cholera in the yard at the rear of the Coach and Horses pub. There were 39 inhabitants in the yard who were drinking from a well contaminated with sewage. Fifteen people contracted the disease and nine of them died. This is the well believed to be concerned. It is adjacent to Cary's wine bar in Dig Street **(top right)**. The late Capt Holland of Ashbourne Hall had been "zealous in advocating a pure supply of water" prior to his death in 1861 and this pump was erected in his memory. When the town water supply was eventually provided in 1896, all the pumps were removed with the exception of this one, presumably out of deference to Capt Holland. It may still be seen on Belle View Road at Dove House Green **(opposite)**.

Fresh water was never quite the same problem in Buxton. Here visitors could sample the mineral water in the Pump Room. Provision for poor people was made at St Anne's Well where they could obtain it freely. However they had to wait until 1840 before it was provided in the much higher Market Place. Even today, St Anne's Well is regularly used by local people filling bottles of the famed mineral water **(top left)**.

Here are views of some of the more unusual troughs which used to supply local villages:

Eyam had one of the oldest village systems in the country, dating from 1588 and these two troughs near to the church were part of it **(opposite top)**. Near to Crag Hall, Wildboarclough are these troughs, arranged in a semi-circle **(opposite bottom)**. On the drive to Gradbach Mill is this trough with a seat on each side **(above)**. **Top** is High Well situated high above Taddington village just off the road to Monyash. It was restored about ten years ago.

In the days before today's preventive medicines, disease was far more common and occasional pitiful stories of the plague and its consequences survive. Eyam is perhaps the best known local example, because of the terrible toll in human misery when 257 people died. Affected communities still needed to live and work, however. Food and other provisions would be left at a certain spot and the money for payment left in vinegar, ostensibly to purify it. Such places were often marked by a stone, such as Mompesson's Well, Eyam (**opposite top**). There are many reminders of the plague. Bodies were often interred away from the community and there must be many that still lie unmarked, hastily buried to prevent the spread of infection. Some are marked, such as the Cundy Graves at Curbar, which date from 1632 (**above**) and the Riley Graves (which contain the Hancock family) at Eyam (**opposite below**). The Eyam plague dates from 1665-6. A further, little known, group of gravestones attributed to this plague exists at the old Bretton Farm, now a youth hostel. They were apparently victims from the families of Morton, Hall and Townsend at Bretton. There is another group situated near to the Bow Stones, south of Lyme Hall in the west of the Peak. These relate to the victims of a plague which swept the area in 1646, but most of the stones have now been removed. The surviving stones are difficult to find and not on a public footpath. They are situated north of the Bow Stones.

Another plague stone survives at Leek near to the Britannia Building Society Head Office, at Birchall (**opposite left**). The Dipping Stone at Whaley Moor, Whaley Bridge may have had a use similar to Mompesson's Well at Eyam (**opposite right**).

Youlgreave had its private water supply until 1998. This stone tank (**above**) was built in 1829 and is known as The Fountain. It provided the village with a head of water, the supply coming from Bradford Dale. The capacity of the tank is 1500 gallons; it is nine feet high and nine feet wide, but has not been used for a long time.

This elegant building (**opposite above**) used to be the offices of a demolished mill at Wildboarclough. It later was used as the village post office and was described as the largest one in the country!

Victorian postboxes are not common in the area. This one, of 1867, survives opposite the Opera House in Buxton **(left)**. One of the largest parishes was Hartington. It was divided into four townships: Upper Hartington Quarter, Middle Hartington Quarter, Town Quarter, and Nether Quarter. This stone **(below right)** is uncommon as it marks the boundary between two townships: Upper and Middle Hartington Quarters. It is on the side of the A515 near Pomeroy near the lane to Chelmorton.

This stone **(below left)** is probably the only remaining sign of the former parish of Beresford. The stone is marked A (on the back) and B and was on the boundary between Alstonfield and Beresford. It is near Endon Cottage in Beresford Lane, near Hulme End.

Two of the former Co-op shops: Hartington (which is still a shop) and Youlgreave **(right)** now a Youth Hostel.

The Hartington Shop **(above)** had a dual purpose as a pub — The Volunteer Arms — but the licence was revoked in 1909. In 1839, three people lost their lives when a barrel of gunpowder ignited at the rear of the shop.

The three-storey building on the left of the photograph used to be a bank.

Pinfolds were used to pen livestock which had been found straying. Not many now survive. Above **(top)** is Biggin pinfold with Hathersage, situated in Church Lane **(above)**. Opposite **(top)** is Curbar, situated on the side of the road to Curbar

Gap. It is opposite the aptly named Pinfold Hill. Curbar Well, is at the top of
Pinfold Hill (where there is this unusual covered well and the circular trough).
The other stones are millstones sunk into the ground **(above)**.

An ancient custom

This is Bosley Cloud, north of Rudyard Lake on the west side of the Peak. On 21st June and the day either side of it, people gather at the rear of the Parish Church in Leek in the hope of seeing a double sunset. The sun sets behind Bosley Cloud and then reappears to the right of the escarpment, to reset below the Cheshire Plain. You have to be lucky, for the event is often marred by cloud or haze.

A fascinating example of the old strip system exists in the ridge and furrow marks which survive alongside the A515 at Tissington. The characteristic ridge and furrow profile comes from ploughing in different directions, throwing the soil over towards the middle of the strip. The ploughman turned his horse around at the end of the strip giving the 's' shape seen here.

The field patterns now preserved by countless stone walls often retain the outline of farming techniques of long ago. At Roystone Grange, north-east of Ashbourne, some of the walls are considered to date from Roman times. Many of the walls are on the boundaries of strips from the old strip system of farming. One field **(above)** between Biggin and Hartington and near Heathcote Mere is two strips wide, both strips being in occupation before the walls were built and appearing on William Senior's plan of the Chatsworth estate dated 1614.

Various narrow strips were amalgamated at Longnor and they can be clearly seen on this photograph **(top)**.

The Manifold Valley contains some good examples of strip lynchets — although they are by no means confined to this area. Experts seem to have differing opinions on the age of these terraces which were used for agricultural purposes. This group is situated to the west of Throwley Hall and can be clearly seen as a group of parallel lines in the middle of the photograph **(above)**. They could be a thousand years or even much older in age.

Chelmorton is well known for visual reminders of its past. Not only are there the numerous walls which marked the consolidation of the narrow strip system into slightly larger units, but at the inner, village end of the strips, the new owners built their houses creating the elongated pattern of the village which we can see today **(opposite above)**.

Near the strip lynchets at Throwley **(see previous page)** are the remains of Throwley Hall of Elizabethan age. It is a pity that a house like this was allowed to deteriorate to this extent **(opposite below)**. This building **(above)**, reminiscent of a Rhineland Castle, is Alton Castle. It was rebuilt in the 1840's by AWN Pugin but some remnants of the Norman original survive. It is a now a private school. The building in the foreground is the lodge to Alton Towers.

What is in a Name?

Flash gave its name to the expression Flash money. Counterfeit money was either made here or at least used by people from here. The village is close to the border with two other counties, Cheshire and Derbyshire, and it was easy to avoid the law by crossing over to another county where the law officers had no jurisdiction. The pub sign **(opposite above)** records that the village is the highest in England.

The Flying Childers Inn at Stanton-in-the-Peak **(opposite below)**. The horse on the inn sign is a give away for the story behind this name. Flying Childers was purchased by the Duke of Devonshire at Newmarket in 1712. It became so famous that a race named after it is still run at Doncaster each year. The oldest racing colours in the country are those of the Duke.

The Via Gellia gave its name to Vyella, the fabric, which used to be manufactured here at Via Gellia Mill **(above top)**. The Green Man and Black's Head Royal Hotel has the most words in any pub name in the country. It is in St John Street, Ashbourne. The gallows-type inn sign is the only one in the Peak **(right)**.

In periods of prolonged dry weather, the water level in Ladybower Reservoir drops sufficiently to reveal the remains of Derwent village. **Above** are the remains of the Hall. Notice the former pond in the left mid-distance. The church was situated in the far distance beyond the pond. Upstream from Derwent was Water House Farm and the remains of this may also be seen under drought conditions. Incredibly, the layout of the garden remains intact too, as may be seen (**opposite**).

Alstonfield Workhouse **(opposite below)** was built around 1790 and survived until 1870, when it was incorporated into the Ashbourne Workhouse (now St Oswald's Hospital). The regime in these establishments was hard and meant to be a deterrent. They were abolished in 1948 and were more common in the towns than in rural areas but others existed in the Peak at Brassington and Bakewell **(opposite above)**.

Hospitals for the working classes became widespread during the nineteenth century. Buxton hospital **(above)** had been built between 1785-90 as a stable block for the hotel patrons at The Crescent. In 1859, it was converted to the Devonshire Royal Hospital 'for the use of the sick poor'. The building had a circular courtyard with a colonnade supported by large Tuscan columns. Here horses were exercised when it was a stable. In 1881, this courtyard was covered by a dome. At the time, it was the largest unsupported dome in the world, weighing 560 tons.

Churches and Chapels

There are no significant monastic remains in the Peak, but the remains of the Cistercian Croxden Abbey **(above)** are worth examining and are only a few miles south-west of Ashbourne. Approach it from Rocester or Alton. The Cistercian's had two other foundations in North Staffordshire, at Hulton Abbey near Stoke-on-Trent and at Dieulacresse Abbey, Leek. However nothing remains of these.

It is hard to appreciate that grave robbers were once a profound pest. This is a watch house (**opposite**), built to deter them and is at High Bradfield, in the Loxley Valley, west of Sheffield.

Ashbourne's Parish Church has the oldest dated brass plaque in the country. It records the reopening of the church following extensions, in 1241 **(opposite below)**.

There are now only two or three residences in the parish of Nether Haddon and one of these is Haddon Hall **(left)**.

The chapel here, on the right hand corner, was the parish church for the village which existed on the sloping ground just to the north of the Hall carpark.

This chapel **(below)** was built by the owner of Belmont Hall, following a dispute with the vicar of Ipstones near Leek. Chapel House is now a private dwelling, but retains its tower and east window.

Hassop (**opposite**) has an unusual church, built in a severe Classical style. Its columns must be missed by many motorists travelling through the village on the main road. Edensor church (**above**) was rebuilt along with the village on a position out of sight of Chatsworth House. It has much of interest, including a display on the rebuilding of the village. Several of the Dukes of Devonshire are buried here and there are quite a few memorials of interest.

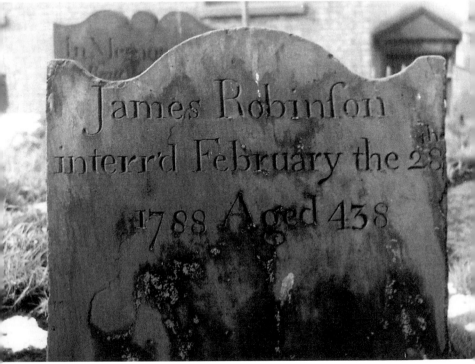

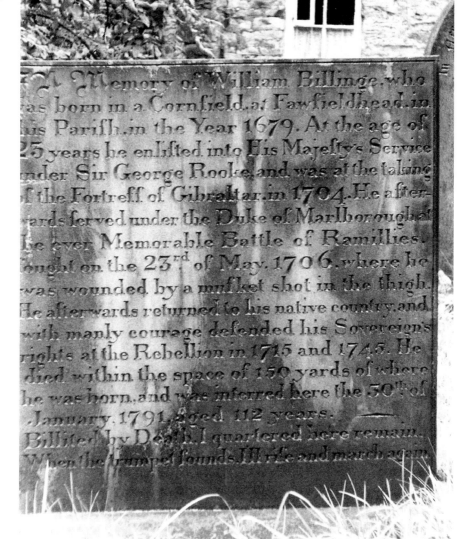

In Memory of William Billinge, who was born in a Cornfield at Fawfieldhead in this Parish in the Year 1679. At the age of 25 years he enlisted into His Majesty's Service under Sir George Rooke, and was at the taking of the Fortress of Gibraltar in 1704. He afterwards served under the Duke of Marlborough at the ever Memorable Battle of Ramillies, fought on the 23rd of May, 1706, where he was wounded by a musket shot in the thigh. He afterwards returned to his native country, and with manly courage defended his Sovereign's rights at the Rebellion in 1715 and 1745. He died within the space of 150 yards of where he was born, and was interred here the 30th of January, 1791, aged 112 years. —

Billited by Death I quartered here remain.
When the trumpet sounds I'll rise and march again.

John Little was a nailer of Hathersage. His cottage is supposed to have existed to the east of the church and to have survived into the 19th Century. He is better known to us all as Little John, the friend of Robin Hood, and his grave may be seen in Hathersage Churchyard (**opposite above**). When opened, a huge thigh bone was reputedly recovered. This stone (**opposite below**) is near to the tower in Leek Parish Churchyard. This surely must stand as the best case of longevity! It is thought that the wrong age was cut and the offending digit filled with lead which has since fallen out. There is no disputing the age or gallantry of William Billinge whose grave (**above**) is at Longnor Church.

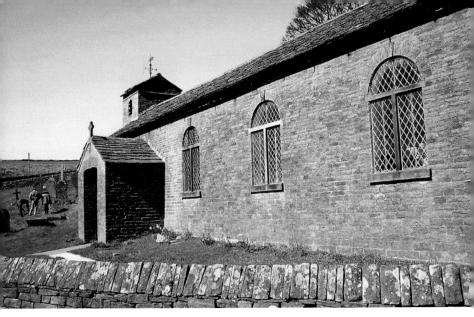

Forest Chapel, near Macclesfield Forest **(top)**. The old Rush Bearing Service is still held here on the Sunday nearest the 12th August. The floor is strewn with rushes prior to the service.

Jenkin Chapel **(below)** to the west of the Goyt Valley by the side of the old salt way to Buxton. It was built in 1733 and the tower was added in 1755. It looks secular, and the small interior, with its box pews has a homely feel to it. There is an open air service here on the second Sunday in September at 3pm.

This barn at Alport Castles Farm, Alport Dale near Ladybower Reservoir **(top)**, was first used in 1662 for Nonconformist worship. Its isolated position must have been ideal. An annual "Love Feast" is held here on the first Sunday in July (details from The Manse, Hathersage).

Below, built by John Lomas in his garden in 1801, is Hollinsclough Chapel. He was a jaggerman or packhorse man and a packhorse way comes down from Axe Edge past the chapel.

One of the finest marble carvings in the churches of the Peak must be this one **(above)** carved by Sir Francis Chantrey in 1826 and showing David Pike-Watts on his death-bed. He raises himself up to greet his daughter Mary and his grandchildren. It is at Ilam. The Chapel is attached to the rest of the ancient church and architecturally shows no sympathy with the previous style.

Behind Errwood Hall on the moor is this stone built shrine **(above)** to Miss Delores, a Spanish companion to Mrs Grimshawe of the Hall and the governess to the latter's children. It was built in 1889 and is still available for a few moments quiet contemplation. Near the ruins of Errwood Hall is the family burial ground **(left)**. Here lie the remains of the Grimshawe family together with some of their servants and the captain of their yacht, *Marquita.*

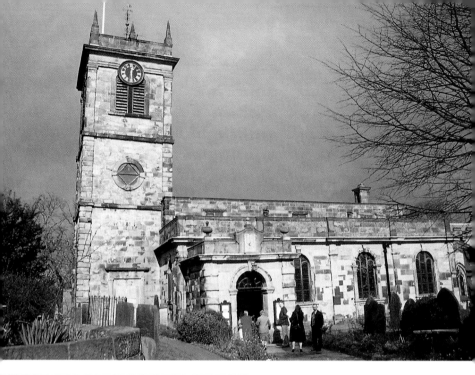

Chapel-en-le-Frith church **(above)** where hundreds of Scottish prisoners were incarcerated during the Civil War. Nearly 50 of them died before they were allowed out. Penistone Church **(left)** is the last resting place for many men who died from cholera in 1849 and accidents from the construction of the Woodhead Tunnel. More were laid to rest here following the building of the Woodhead reservoirs. Other burials from accidents were made in neighbouring churches too. The working conditions on the Woodhead Tunnel were disgraceful. The work was dangerous through poor working practices and the social conditions for the men were little better, although the cholera was brought to the site from elsewhere.

This sensitive carving by Thomas Banks of Penelope Boothby **(top)** is to be found in Ashbourne Church. It was carved in 1793. She was painted by Reynolds in 1791 and this was copied by Millais later under the title *The Mop Cap*. Many Victorian girls went to fancy dress parties dressed as "Penelope", presumably without knowing who she was. This memorial **(below)** to Lord Frederick Cavendish was sent by Queen Victoria following his assasination in Pheonix Park, Dublin, in 1882.

Charles Cotton's pew at Alstonfield Church. It was unfortunately painted green in the 19th century. Cotton lived a little to the north of the village at the now demolished Beresford Hall.

Alstonfield also has a most unusual double-decker pulpit.

The Cavendish Memorial at Edensor. This huge piece dates from the 17th Century and commemorates William, First Duke of Devonshire and Henry Cavendish. It is in the same chapel as the memorial to Lord Frederick Cavendish.

Padley Chapel, the sole remnant of Padley Hall, built in the 14th and 15th Centuries. The FitzHerberts who lived at the Hall were Catholics and two priests were arrested here in 1588. They were hung, drawn and quartered at Derby. The chapel was restored in 1933. A remembrance service for the Padley Martyrs is held here annually on the Thursday nearest 12th July. The excavated remains of the Hall are behind the chapel.

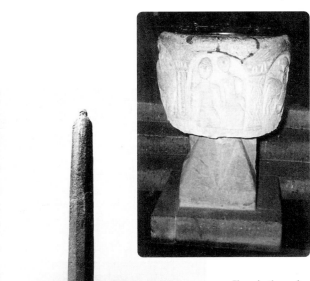

Saxon architecture is not very common in the Peak. Here is a doorway at Ilam **(top left)**. This church also has a Saxon font (inset). A lovely early 9th Century cross may be seen at Eyam Church **(top right)**. Part of the shaft is missing. This preaching cross **(left)** stands in an isolated position above Stile House Farm on the side of Morridge, overlooking Leek.

Ilam is the only church in the Peak to contain the grave of a saint: St Bertram **(opposite above)**. Only the foundations of Derwent Church remain and these are flooded under Ladybower Reservoir unless there is extreme drought. One of the remaining stones bears the date of construction, 1867 **(opposite below)**.

This collection of maidens' garlands **(above)** may be seen at Matlock Church, although the latter is kept locked. They were usually left at the church when a young woman died and there are more at Ashford-in-the-Water and Ilam. This wonderful sundial dates from 1775 and may be seen at Eyam Church **(below)**.

The Church clock at Baslow (**above**) does not have numbers but spells VICTO-RIA 1897. It commemorates the Queen's 60th Jubilee. This is Hathersage Rectory (**below**), where Charlotte Bronë stayed in 1845. *Jane Eyre* was based upon this area and her friends, the Nussey's who lived there. In fact Henry Nussey, the brother of her friend Ellen, proposed to her, which may have been in Charlotte's mind as she wrote her bestseller. In the book, Hathersage is called *Morten*.

PEAK DISTRICT
SECRETS AND CURIOSITIES

Home and Village Life;
Churches and Chapels

At Work; On the Road;
Railways and Canals

Natural Features;
Memorials and Monuments;
Stocks and Lock ups;
Follies, Towers and
Unusual Buildings

Learn much more about the Peak District by buying these three lovely books. They are ideal as a gift, a souvenir or as a source of reference about the Peak.

If you would like to complete your set, photocopy the order form below or order direct from your bookshop.

Please send me:—

Peak District Secrets & Curiosities

Vol 1	£3.95	☐
Vol 2	£3.95	☐
Vol 3	£3.95	☐

Please add 75p per book for postage. Send this form together with your cheque, payable to Ashbourne Editions, to Sprinkswood, Clifton, Ashbourne, Derbyshire, DE6 2GL.

Name	
Address	